I AM

Discovering Who Jesus Is

8 studies
for individuals or groups

Douglas Connelly

With Notes for Leaders

IV

An in
Downers ....

InterVarsity Press
P.O. Box 1400, Downers Grove, IL 60515-1426
World Wide Web: www.ivpress.com
E-mail: email@ivpress.com

InterVarsity Press® is the book-publishing division of InterVarsity Christian Fellowship/USA®, a student
movement active on campus at hundreds of universities, colleges and schools of nursing in the United
States of America, and a member movement of the International Fellowship of Evangelical Students. For
information about local and regional activities, write Public Relations Dept., InterVarsity Christian
Fellowship/USA, 6400 Schroeder Rd., P.O. Box 7895, Madison, WI 53707-7895, or visit the IVCF website
at <www.intervarsity.org>.

LifeGuide® is a registered trademark of InterVarsity Christian Fellowship.

All Scripture quotations, unless otherwise indicated, are taken from the Holy Bible, New International
Version®. NIV®. Copyright ©1973, 1978, 1984 by International Bible Society. Used by permission of
Zondervan Publishing House. All rights reserved.

Cover image: Urmas Ääro/istockphoto.com
      flames: Brian Gordon Green/National Geographic Image Collection

ISBN 978-0-8308-3133-3

Printed in the United States of America ∞

P	18	17	16	15	14	13	12	11	10	9	8	7	6	5	4	3	2	1
Y	22	21	20	19	18	17	16	15	14	13	12	11	10	09	08	07

Contents

Getting the Most Out of
I Am

No one could say the things Jesus said and be taken seriously.

Imagine standing up in an office meeting or even at a small group Bible study and saying: "I am the way; no one has access to God except through me." Or think about how you would react if someone took the microphone at a funeral and announced: "I am the resurrection and the life; if you believe in me, you will never die." That person would be asked to sit down—or ushered out the door! No one would take such claims seriously.

But those are the very words we hear from Jesus in the Bible—and from Jesus the words ring true. Who is this man who makes such sweeping claims? And how can such a man bring rest to my restless spirit?

The claims Jesus made sounded even more startling to the people who first heard them. The words "I am" drew Jesus' first-century Jewish audience back to a pivotal point in biblical history. God spoke to Moses from a burning bush and sent him to Egypt to lead the people of Israel to freedom. Moses worried that the people would want to know who had sent him and so he asked God what his name was. God answered, "I AM WHO I AM" (Exodus 3:14). God's covenant name with Israel was "I AM." Now, hundreds of years later, the same words come from the lips of Jesus. He is claiming to be no one less than the Lord God. The same God who spoke to Moses now speaks again.

This study guide examines the "I AM" declarations of Jesus

in the New Testament. We will look at the context of each statement, and we will listen to Jesus' powerful words—but we want to go beyond simply a study of ancient words. We will also discover how Jesus' words can transform our lives today. Be prepared to wrestle with some amazing claims. Then be prepared to have your life changed as Jesus' claims ring true in your experience.

Suggestions for Individual Study

1. As you begin each study, pray that God will speak to you through his Word.

2. Read the introduction to the study and respond to the personal reflection question or exercise. This is designed to help you focus on God and on the theme of the study.

3. Each study deals with a particular passage—so that you can delve into the author's meaning in that context. Read and reread the passage to be studied. The questions are written using the language of the New International Version, so you may wish to use that version of the Bible. The New Revised Standard Version is also recommended.

4. This is an inductive Bible study, designed to help you discover for yourself what Scripture is saying. The study includes three types of questions. *Observation* questions ask about the basic facts: who, what, when, where and how. *Interpretation* questions delve into the meaning of the passage. *Application* questions help you discover the implications of the text for growing in Christ. These three keys unlock the treasures of Scripture.

Write your answers to the questions in the spaces provided or in a personal journal. Writing can bring clarity and deeper understanding of yourself and of God's Word.

5. It might be good to have a Bible dictionary handy. Use it to look up any unfamiliar words, names or places.

6. Use the prayer suggestion to guide you in thanking God for what you have learned and to pray about the applications that have come to mind.

7. You may want to go on to the suggestion under "Now or Later," or you may want to use that idea for your next study.

Suggestions for Members of a Group Study

1. Come to the study prepared. Follow the suggestions for individual study mentioned above. You will find that careful preparation will greatly enrich your time spent in group discussion.

2. Be willing to participate in the discussion. The leader of your group will not be lecturing. Instead, he or she will be encouraging the members of the group to discuss what they have learned. The leader will be asking the questions that are found in this guide.

3. Stick to the topic being discussed. Your answers should be based on the verses which are the focus of the discussion and not on outside authorities such as commentaries or speakers. These studies focus on a particular passage of Scripture. Only rarely should you refer to other portions of the Bible. This allows for everyone to participate in in-depth study on equal ground.

4. Be sensitive to the other members of the group. Listen attentively when they describe what they have learned. You may be surprised by their insights! Each question assumes a variety of answers. Many questions do not have "right" answers, particularly questions that aim at meaning or application. Instead the questions push us to explore the passage more thoroughly.

When possible, link what you say to the comments of others. Also, be affirming whenever you can. This will encourage some of the more hesitant members of the group to participate.

5. Be careful not to dominate the discussion. We are sometimes so eager to express our thoughts that we leave too little opportunity for others to respond. By all means participate! But allow others to also.

6. Expect God to teach you through the passage being discussed and through the other members of the group. Pray that you will have an enjoyable and profitable time together, but also that as a result of the study you will find ways that you can take action individually and/or as a group.

7. Remember that anything said in the group is considered confidential and should not be discussed outside the group unless specific permission is given to do so.

8. If you are the group leader, you will find additional suggestions at the back of the guide.

1

I Am He

Salvation

"Do you know anything about the Bible?" I was browsing the religion section of the local bookstore, and a woman of Middle Eastern descent startled me with her question. "There are so many Bibles here," she said, "and I don't know which one to choose."

I asked a few questions and made a couple recommendations. When she walked away with her new Bible, she smiled and thanked me for helping her. "American men," she whispered, "are not usually so polite."

Her words still ring in my mind. I wonder how often she has been scorned or ignored. I wonder if any Christians have crossed the path of her life and how they have treated her.

GROUP DISCUSSION. How do you respond when someone speaks to you unexpectedly? Share a story if you have one.

PERSONAL REFLECTION. What kind of person are you reluctant or afraid to speak to? What factors make you hesitant?

Jesus made some amazing claims about himself—and often to the most unexpected people! In John 4 Jesus reveals himself as the source of eternal life to a woman no one else would talk to. *Read John 4:1-26.*

1. The Jewish people of Jesus' day despised the Samaritans (and the Samaritans returned the favor). Trying to think from that cultural background, how would you feel upon hearing that Jesus had decided to go through Samaria rather than taking the longer, but more acceptable, way around the territory?

2. What barriers is Jesus willing to overcome in order to have a conversation with the Samaritan woman?

3. What barriers hinder Christians today from engaging others in conversation about Jesus?

4. What does Jesus mean when he offers her "living water" (vv. 10, 13-14)?

What does the woman think Jesus means (vv. 11-12, 15)?

5. Why does Jesus bring up the woman's past marriages and present adulterous relationship (vv. 16-18)?

6. Why do you think the woman makes the comments in verses 19-20?

How does Jesus respond (vv. 21-24)?

7. What does it mean to worship God "in spirit and in truth" (vv. 23-24)?

8. In verses 25 and 26 Jesus clearly claims to be the Messiah, the deliverer God had promised to send. Imagine the look on the woman's face when she hears his words. Do you think she is surprised or skeptical, and why?

9. What does Jesus' offer of living water mean in your life and spiritual experience?

Identify any fears or prejudices that may keep you from talking to other people about Jesus. Ask God to give you the courage to overcome those barriers.

Now or Later

What would Jesus talk with you about if you had a quiet lunch together? In a journal or the space here, formulate two or three issues that you think Jesus might want to address.

How would you respond—by changing the subject or by receiving his grace? Prayerfully talk over those issues with Jesus. Listen for his response.

2

I Am the Bread of Life

Survival

John 6:25-51

We love to eat—on holidays we do it all day long! The people in Jesus' day loved to eat as well. The one fact about eating that we learn very quickly is that, even if we eat until we are full, a few hours later we are hungry again.

GROUP DISCUSSION. Talk about your favorite food or favorite restaurant. How do you feel after you have eaten what you enjoy?

PERSONAL REFLECTION. What do you "hunger" for in your life? What desires never seem to be satisfied?

One day Jesus feeds a throng of people by multiplying a few small loaves of bread and a couple dried fish (John 6:1-14)—but the next day the people are hungry again! Jesus tries to point them (and us) to spiritual nourishment that satisfies our hearts forever. *Read John 6:25-51.*

---

1. Do you think the crowd is favorable to Jesus or hostile to him? Explain your answer based on statements from the passage.

---

2. Jesus contrasts two appetites—one for physical nourishment and one for spiritual sustenance. How is each appetite satisfied (vv. 26-27)?

---

3. When the crowd asks how they can please God and do God's will, Jesus says, "Believe in the one he has sent" (v. 29). But their response is to ask for a miracle (v. 30). How is their response similar to the response of our culture to the claims of Christ?

---

4. How would you explain what Jesus means when he says, "I am the bread of life" (v. 35; see also vv. 27 and 33)?

Do you think the crowd understands what Jesus is saying? Why or why not?

5. How would you describe your daily spiritual diet: healthy and nourishing, junk food, starvation level, same old reheated food? Explain the results of this diet in your spiritual life as a whole.

6. What does Jesus promise to those who come to him in faith for spiritual nourishment (vv. 37-40)?

7. How does the crowd's understanding of where Jesus came from parallel what they thought about Jesus' offer of bread (vv. 41-42)?

8. Jesus makes some startling claims in this passage: to satisfy our deepest needs and desires, to come from God the Father, to preserve us as his children, to raise our bodies from the dead on the last day, to be the source of eternal life. How do these claims compare with what most people in our society believe about Jesus?

---

9. What does Jesus want the people in the crowd (or people reading this account today) to conclude about who he is?

Reaffirm your personal response of faith and trust in Jesus. Thank him for satisfying all your spiritual longings and needs.

Now or Later

All of us have to spend time and energy meeting our physical and financial needs. How balanced is your effort to meet your spiritual needs? Ask a Christian friend to help you evaluate your spiritual growth. Take one step this week to bring greater balance between your search for physical bread and your pursuit of Christ, your spiritual bread.

3

I Am the Light

Direction

John 8:12-30

When I was a boy, my parents took me on a tour of a cavern in Pennsylvania. I got bored with the tour director's long commentary on every formation, so I decided to walk ahead and see what was around the next curve in the path. What I didn't know was that the tour guide was about to demonstrate how dark the cavern was when all the lights were turned off. I can still remember the icy fingers of the absolute darkness gripping me in terror.

GROUP DISCUSSION. What is your most vivid memory involving a dark place?

PERSONAL REFLECTION. What feelings do you associate with darkness? Why?

Jesus was not afraid to defend the truth even in the face of his enemies. In this passage Jesus makes a series of claims that his opponents try to challenge. Jesus' response to their opposition leads each time to a new claim about Jesus' power or origin. *Read John 8:12-30.*

---

1. What does it feel like to walk in darkness (v. 12)?

How have you experienced following Jesus as being like following a light through a dark place?

---

2. Biblical law required that a person's testimony had to be verified by the testimony of others. (See Deuteronomy 19:15, for example.) The religious teachers try to use that requirement to challenge Jesus' claim to be the light of the world (v. 13). How does Jesus answer their challenge (vv. 14-18)?

---

3. Why do *you* believe the testimony of Jesus that he came from the Father?

4. What does the Pharisees' misunderstanding in verse 19 reveal about their view of Jesus?

---

5. In verse 24 Jesus says, "If you do not believe that I am the one I claim to be, you will indeed die in your sins." How does our contemporary culture respond to that claim?

---

6. Why would Jesus' opponents only realize who he was when they had "lifted up the Son of Man" (vv. 27-28)?

---

7. What is your testimony about Jesus to the people you work with or spend time with?

What would they say about the validity of your testimony?

8. Jesus said, "I always do what pleases [the Father]" (v. 29). Should that be a goal in your life? Explain why or why not.

9. How can you rely on Jesus as your "light" this week?

What can you expect, and how will you respond to his light?

Make me willing, Lord, to follow your light and to walk in it.

Now or Later

Take a late night walk. Bring a flashlight and think about the world we live in as the realm of spiritual darkness. What does Jesus, the light, provide to us as we walk? What happens if you lay the light down and leave it behind?

4

I Am the
Good Shepherd

Security

Shepherds in the ancient world had a close bond with their sheep. Lambs were raised almost like children with plenty of hugs and affection. The shepherd would call his sheep by name and the sheep would follow him because they knew that protection and nourishment came from the shepherd's skillful care. The sheep also responded to the shepherd's voice because they knew he loved them and that he was concerned for their well-being. Security and satisfaction came from staying close to the shepherd.

GROUP DISCUSSION. What person in your family or circle of friends makes you feel most secure and loved? What does that person do to convey their affection?

PERSONAL REFLECTION. In what circumstances do you feel most insecure or afraid? Who do you turn to when you feel that way?

Jesus uses the familiar image of a shepherd and his sheep to illustrate his love for his followers and our value to him. We are his prized possession—a possession he guides and protects and cares for, just as a shepherd nurtures his flock of sheep. Jesus' words bring comfort and assurance to people who live in a very threatening and insecure world. *Read John 10:1-21.*

1. As you scan back through the passage, list all the things that the shepherd does for the sheep.

Which of these do you think is most important in the person who "shepherds" your life, and why?

2. What responsibilities are placed on the sheep in this passage?

3. Who or what is represented by the thief or the wolf in Jesus' story?

Compare the goals of the thief and the wolf with the goals of the shepherd.

4. Several times Jesus says that the good shepherd lays down his life for the sheep (vv. 11, 15, 17-18). How does Jesus' sacrifice of himself make you feel about yourself? How does it make you feel about Jesus?

5. Why does Jesus emphasize that he lays down his life of his own accord (vv. 17-18)?

6. How do Jesus' listeners respond to his words (vv. 6, 19-21)?

Why do you think his words create such a difference of opinion?

7. How do people respond today to Jesus' gracious offer to be their shepherd?

8. Even under the watchful eye of a shepherd, sheep can wander off. In what situations have you left (or been tempted to leave) the safety of Jesus' care?

What is the good shepherd's response to us when we wander off?

9. What have you learned about Jesus in this passage that will help you when you (or a friend) struggle with accepting Jesus' love?

Ask the Lord to shield your life with confidence and security in Jesus' love for you.

Now or Later

The best-known passage in the Bible that pictures God's care as a shepherd for his people is Psalm 23. Read the psalm carefully and list all the things that the shepherd does for his sheep. Recast those promises in your own words to reflect what Jesus, the Good Shepherd, does in your life.

5

I Am the Resurrection

Eternity

John 11:1-27

The other day I stood at the casket of a man who had lived more than one hundred years. He saw one century of time pass! I had no doubts about his destiny. He had believed in Jesus as a young man and had given evidence of his faith through a long life of commitment to Christ. What I wondered about, however, was what that journey from the darkness of death to the daybreak of heaven was like.

GROUP DISCUSSION. Think about a time when you prayed intently for someone close to you but did not receive the answer you asked for. How did that experience make you feel at the time about God?

PERSONAL REFLECTION. If you could get one answer from God about death or life after death, what question would you ask?

Jesus often confronted death and the pain it brings into our lives. In this passage he comes to a grieving woman with a startling word of hope. *Read John 11:1-27.*

1. From what you have read in this passage, how would you describe the relationship between Jesus and Martha?

Between Jesus and Lazarus?

2. What risk was Jesus taking by going back to Judea (vv. 8, 16)?

3. How would you feel if your closest friend did not come when you needed him or her most?

4. What do you think Martha had in mind when she said, "I know that even now God will give you whatever you ask" (v. 22)?

5. What situations may cause us to be disappointed with God?

---

6. What does Jesus mean when he says the person who believes in him will live, even though he dies (v. 25)?

---

7. Now look again at verse 26. Can those who believe in Jesus expect that they will never die? Explain what Jesus means.

---

8. If Jesus is the resurrection and the life, how would you describe the life we have right now when we believe in him?

---

9. What assurance do Jesus' words give you about your death and life beyond death?

10. What "deathlike" situations in your life can Jesus' resurrection power change?

How will Jesus' words change the way you pray for those who are going through a difficult time?

Thank Jesus for his life-giving power and commit any impossible situations to him.

Now or Later

Focus on a specific need or relationship in your life that you want God to change. Write that need in a journal or on the back pages of your Bible. Begin to pray for resurrection power in that situation. Keep a record of how God works and the time frame he chooses to use.

6

I Am the Way

Peace

In our church we invite people with pressing needs to come to the altar for prayer. Every week the altar is lined with people who have troubled hearts. Other Christians pray with them and for them. Our cry is that Jesus will touch us and that we will receive his peace.

GROUP DISCUSSION. Who do you want to be around when you are hurting or distressed? How does that person bring comfort to you?

PERSONAL REFLECTION. What is troubling your heart right now?

Jesus' followers felt like their world was falling apart. Jesus had just told them that he was leaving and they couldn't come with him. The path to the cross was for Jesus alone. In the backwash of their sorrow and distress, Jesus speaks words of peace—and makes an astonishing claim! *Read John 14:1-14.*

---

1. Think about times of stress and sorrow in your life, and then consider what the disciples were feeling. What is it like to have a "troubled" heart?

---

2. What will Jesus be doing when he leaves his disciples (vv. 2-4)?

---

3. In what ways is Jesus preparing you to be with him in the Father's house?

---

4. What does Thomas's question tell you about what was troubling his heart (v. 5)?

5. How is Jesus' claim to be "the way and the truth and the life" received in our society?

---

6. How would you answer the person who thinks it is narrow and intolerant to believe that Jesus is the only way to God?

---

7. Put Jesus' response to Philip's question in your own words (vv. 9-10). What is Jesus saying about who he is?

---

8. In what ways did the disciples (or Christians today) do "greater things" than what Jesus did (v. 12)?

---

9. Is verse 13 a "blank check" to get anything we want from God? Explain your answer.

10. What can you learn from this passage that will help you to "stop having a troubled heart"?

Pray Jesus' promises over the things that are troubling you.

Now or Later

Think of a person you know who needs to believe in Jesus as the way to God and the life of God. Begin to pray for that person. Ask God to give you an opportunity to talk with that person about your own faith in Jesus. Look for God-appointed openings to begin a discussion with that person about spiritual issues. You might want to share that person's name with another believer so you can pray together. Claim Jesus' promise that, what you ask in his name, he will do.

7

I Am the True Vine

Purpose

I drove through the vineyards of Western Michigan early one spring and was shocked to see how drastically the workers were pruning the grapevines. The plants looked like bleeding stumps! When I asked why they cut the vines back so severely, one vineyard owner made the reason very clear. "You have to choose," he said, "between beautiful, leafy vines or plump, juicy grapes."

GROUP DISCUSSION. How are you at getting plants to grow? Tell a story of a memorable plant experience.

PERSONAL REFLECTION. If you picture your life as a plant, what condition are you in: pretty healthy, a little undernourished, dry and brittle, or ready to be transplanted?

Jesus spoke the words of John 15 as he and his closest follow-ers made their way from a banquet room in Jerusalem to an olive grove on the slopes of the Mount of Olives. Maybe they were walking through a grape vineyard on their way or maybe Jesus pointed to carvings of grapevines on the walls of the tem-ple as they walked through. The imagery of the vine and the branches was a very familiar part of the cultural setting in Jesus' world. *Read John 15:1-8.*

1. In the natural world, what does the main vine do for the smaller branches?

What benefits do the branches provide to the vine?

2. Jesus uses the vine and branches as an allegory of the rela-tionship he has with his followers. If he is the vine and we are the branches, what does Jesus provide in the relationship?

What do we as branches provide for Jesus the vine?

3. God the Father is the overseer and caretaker of the relation-ship between Jesus and his followers. How does he tend to the branches that bear fruit and to the branches that do not (v. 2)?

4. What is the "fruit" that the Father desires to see in our lives?

Take a few moments to reflect quietly before you respond: What specifically do you think is the fruit the Father desires for you?

---

5. Jesus repeatedly calls us to "remain" or "abide" in him. What does that mean?

What are the consequences of not remaining in him?

---

6. How might the Father "prune" our lives to prompt us to produce more fruit?

---

7. How does this passage help you understand God's purposes for the difficult pruning experiences in your life?

8. Based on this passage, how would you explain to a friend what your purpose in life really is?

---

9. What specific steps can you take to remind yourself of God's purpose for your life as you go through the routine of your day?

Ask God to help you to understand and accept the pruning of your life. Ask him to give you a vision of what he desires you to be.

Now or Later

Jesus says that people who remain in him can ask whatever they wish and it will be given to them (v. 7)? How does that work? Can I ask for a million dollars and expect a check in the mail?

Does his promise make you more courageous or more conservative in prayer? Explain why.

8

I Am the Alpha and Omega

Confidence

Revelation 1:8; 22:12-16

Most of us are great at starting new projects. We open a new book or start a remodeling project or assemble the new home fitness machine with enthusiasm and determination. Starting projects is not our problem! Where I run into trouble is on the other end—or somewhere in the middle. Finishing that new landscape design or sticking to the diet or actually using the treadmill three times a week is where we struggle.

GROUP DISCUSSION. Tell the group about a project at home or at work that you began and carried through to the end. How did you feel when it was completed?

PERSONAL REFLECTION. When are you most tempted to quit on a difficult project or journey—before you start, halfway through or when you are almost done? What unfinished project would you most like to get done?

In Revelation, Jesus makes an astonishing claim about the biggest endeavor of all time—the entire human story. Jesus says that he was present when it all began and that he will be there when human history comes to a conclusion. He is the first letter of the human saga—the Alpha—and he will be the final letter of the final chapter—the Omega. *Read Revelation 1:8 and 22:12-16.*

---

1. Who is identified as the speaker in Revelation 1:8?

Who speaks in Revelation 22:16?

What conclusion can you draw from that comparison?

---

2. How does the average person respond to Jesus' promises in 22:12 about his return and his reward?

---

3. Do you think Jesus just got things on earth started and will someday wind things up but that he pretty much ignores what is going on in between? Explain your answer.

4. What views have you heard about how human history will end?

How does it make you feel to know that Jesus will be the one who brings the human story to the conclusion he desires?

5. Who are the people who are granted access to the eternal city and the tree of life (v. 14)?

6. What does Jesus' description of those who are excluded from the city tell you about their spiritual condition and relationship with God (v. 15)?

7. How does Jesus' claim to be the sovereign Lord over history—and over your life—help you face the successes and tragedies of your daily experience?

8. As you think back through the claims Jesus has made in these studies, which one has blessed or encouraged you most? Explain why.

9. What difference does knowing who Jesus is make in how we live each day?

Affirm that Jesus is your sovereign Lord and that your desire is to please him in all you do.

Now or Later

Read John's description of heaven in Revelation 21:1-7. What aspect of heaven seems most comforting or appealing to you right now? Why?

Leader's Notes

MY GRACE IS SUFFICIENT FOR YOU. (2 COR 12:9)

Leading a Bible discussion can be an enjoyable and rewarding experience. But it can also be *scary*—especially if you've never done it before. If this is your feeling, you're in good company. When God asked Moses to lead the Israelites out of Egypt, he replied, "O LORD, please send someone else to do it" (Ex 4:13). It was the same with Solomon, Jeremiah and Timothy, but God helped these people in spite of their weaknesses, and he will help you as well.

You don't need to be an expert on the Bible or a trained teacher to lead a Bible discussion. The idea behind these inductive studies is that the leader guides group members to discover for themselves what the Bible has to say. This method of learning will allow group members to remember much more of what is said than a lecture would.

These studies are designed to be led easily. As a matter of fact, the flow of questions through the passage from observation to interpretation to application is so natural that you may feel that the studies lead themselves. This study guide is also flexible. You can use it with a variety of groups—student, professional, neighborhood or church groups. Each study takes forty-five to sixty minutes in a group setting.

There are some important facts to know about group dynamics and encouraging discussion. The suggestions listed below should enable you to effectively and enjoyably fulfill your role as leader.

Preparing for the Study

1. Ask God to help you understand and apply the passage in your

own life. Unless this happens, you will not be prepared to lead others. Pray too for the various members of the group. Ask God to open your hearts to the message of his Word and motivate you to action.

2. Read the introduction to the entire guide to get an overview of the entire book and the issues which will be explored.

3. As you begin each study, read and reread the assigned Bible passage to familiarize yourself with it.

4. This study guide is based on the New International Version of the Bible. It will help you and the group if you use this translation as the basis for your study and discussion.

5. Carefully work through each question in the study. Spend time in meditation and reflection as you consider how to respond.

6. Write your thoughts and responses in the space provided in the study guide. This will help you to express your understanding of the passage clearly.

7. It might help to have a Bible dictionary handy. Use it to look up any unfamiliar words, names or places. (For additional help on how to study a passage, see chapter five of *How to Lead a LifeGuide Bible Study*, InterVarsity Press.)

8. Consider how you can apply the Scripture to your life. Remember that the group will follow your lead in responding to the studies. They will not go any deeper than you do.

9. Once you have finished your own study of the passage, familiarize yourself with the leader's notes for the study you are leading. These are designed to help you in several ways. First, they tell you the purpose the study guide author had in mind when writing the study. Take time to think through how the study questions work together to accomplish that purpose. Second, the notes provide you with additional background information or suggestions on group dynamics for various questions. This information can be useful when people have difficulty understanding or answering a question. Third, the leader's notes can alert you to potential problems you may encounter during the study.

10. If you wish to remind yourself of anything mentioned in the leader's notes, make a note to yourself below that question in the study.

Leading the Study

1. Begin the study on time. Open with prayer, asking God to help the group to understand and apply the passage.

2. Be sure that everyone in your group has a study guide. Encourage the group to prepare beforehand for each discussion by reading the introduction to the guide and by working through the questions in the study.

3. At the beginning of your first time together, explain that these studies are meant to be discussions, not lectures. Encourage the members of the group to participate. However, do not put pressure on those who may be hesitant to speak during the first few sessions. You may want to suggest the following guidelines to your group.

☐ Stick to the topic being discussed.

☐ Your responses should be based on the verses which are the focus of the discussion and not on outside authorities such as commentaries or speakers.

☐ These studies focus on a particular passage of Scripture. Only rarely should you refer to other portions of the Bible. This allows for everyone to participate in in-depth study on equal ground.

☐ Anything said in the group is considered confidential and will not be discussed outside the group unless specific permission is given to do so.

☐ We will listen attentively to each other and provide time for each person present to talk.

☐ We will pray for each other.

4. Have a group member read the introduction at the beginning of the discussion.

5. Every session begins with a group discussion question. The question or activity is meant to be used before the passage is read. The question introduces the theme of the study and encourages group members to begin to open up. Encourage as many members as possible to participate, and be ready to get the discussion going with your own response.

This section is designed to reveal where our thoughts or feelings need to be transformed by Scripture. That is why it is especially important not to read the passage before the discussion question is asked. The passage will tend to color the honest reactions people would otherwise give because they are, of course, supposed to think the way the Bible does.

You may want to supplement the group discussion question with an icebreaker to help people to get comfortable. See the community section of *Small Group Idea Book* for more ideas.

You also might want to use the personal reflection question with your group. Either allow a time of silence for people to respond individually or discuss it together.

6. Have a group member (or members if the passage is long) read aloud the passage to be studied. Then give people several minutes to read the passage again silently so that they can take it all in.

7. Question 1 will generally be an overview question designed to briefly survey the passage. Encourage the group to look at the whole passage, but try to avoid getting sidetracked by questions or issues that will be addressed later in the study.

8. As you ask the questions, keep in mind that they are designed to be used just as they are written. You may simply read them aloud. Or you may prefer to express them in your own words.

There may be times when it is appropriate to deviate from the study guide. For example, a question may have already been answered. If so, move on to the next question. Or someone may raise an important question not covered in the guide. Take time to discuss it, but try to keep the group from going off on tangents.

9. Avoid answering your own questions. If necessary, repeat or rephrase them until they are clearly understood. Or point out something you read in the leader's notes to clarify the context or meaning. An eager group quickly becomes passive and silent if they think the leader will do most of the talking.

10. Don't be afraid of silence. People may need time to think about the question before formulating their answers.

11. Don't be content with just one answer. Ask, "What do the rest of you think?" or "Anything else?" until several people have given answers to the question.

12. Acknowledge all contributions. Try to be affirming whenever possible. Never reject an answer. If it is clearly off-base, ask, "Which

verse led you to that conclusion?" or again, "What do the rest of you think?"

13. Don't expect every answer to be addressed to you, even though this will probably happen at first. As group members become more at ease, they will begin to truly interact with each other. This is one sign of healthy discussion.

14. Don't be afraid of controversy. It can be very stimulating. If you don't resolve an issue completely, don't be frustrated. Move on and keep it in mind for later. A subsequent study may solve the problem.

15. Periodically summarize what the group has said about the passage. This helps to draw together the various ideas mentioned and gives continuity to the study. But don't preach.

16. At the end of the Bible discussion you may want to allow group members a time of quiet to work on an idea under "Now or Later." Then discuss what you experienced. Or you may want to encourage group members to work on these ideas between meetings. Give an opportunity during the session for people to talk about what they are learning.

17. Conclude your time together with conversational prayer, adapting the prayer suggestion at the end of the study to your group. Ask for God's help in following through on the commitments you've made.

18. End on time.

Many more suggestions and helps are found in *How to Lead a LifeGuide Bible Study*.

Components of Small Groups

A healthy small group should do more than study the Bible. There are four components to consider as you structure your time together.

Nurture. Small groups help us to grow in our knowledge and love of God. Bible study is the key to making this happen and is the foundation of your small group.

Community. Small groups are a great place to develop deep friendships with other Christians. Allow time for informal interaction before and after each study. Plan activities and games that will help you get to know each other. Spend time having fun together—going on a picnic or cooking dinner together.

Worship and prayer. Your study will be enhanced by spending time praising God together in prayer or song. Pray for each other's needs—and keep track of how God is answering prayer in your group. Ask God to help you to apply what you are learning in your study.

Outreach. Reaching out to others can be a practical way of applying what you are learning, and it will keep your group from becoming self-focused. Host a series of evangelistic discussions for your friends or neighbors. Clean up the yard of an elderly friend. Serve at a soup kitchen together, or spend a day working on a Habitat house.

Many more suggestions and helps in each of these areas are found in *Small Group Idea Book.* Information on building a small group can be found in *Small Group Leaders' Handbook* and *The Big Book on Small Groups* (both from InterVarsity Press). Reading through one of these books would be worth your time.

Study 1. I Am He: Salvation. John 4:1-26

Purpose: To understand Jesus' claim to be the Savior and to be prompted to tell other people about his saving grace.

Question 1. The Samaritans were the descendants of Jewish people who intermarried with non-Jewish (Gentile) people. Seven hundred years before Jesus was born, Assyrian armies conquered the northern part of the land of Israel and brought in other conquered peoples from other parts of their empire. These non-Jews intermarried with the Jewish people left in the land after the conquest. Their descendants gradually adopted the Jewish faith but, because they were of mixed racial origin, Samaritans were barred from worship in the temple in Jerusalem. The Samaritans tried to build a rival temple on Mount Gerizim, but the Jews eventually tore it down.

The Samaritans in Jesus' day were looked on as racially impure and theologically suspect. Jews who traveled between Galilee in the north and Judea in the south avoided Samaria by crossing over the Jordan River and traveling through non-Samaritan territory. Jesus deliberately went through Samaria so he could have this encounter at the town of Sychar.

A map showing the main territories and the routes north and

south is located on page 60. You may want to turn there as you give some background to the story. Solicit the group's responses to the question.

Question 2. Beyond the religious barrier and racial barrier, Jesus also crossed the gender barrier (a man speaking to a woman). Pious Jews believed it was inappropriate for a man to address any woman in public, much less a Samaritan woman. Jesus also crossed a moral barrier. He was the Son of God; she was a woman living in an immoral relationship. The woman came to the well at an unusual time. The custom was to draw water early in the morning or in the evening. The woman may have come at noon to avoid the stares and harsh words of others in the village. It also permitted Jesus to speak with her privately but in open view.

Question 3. Draw some contemporary parallels with the situation Jesus faced; then branch out to other barriers that may keep us from talking to someone about Jesus.

Question 4. "Living water" was a common reference to water that flowed, such as water from a spring or even a stream. At the bottom of the well in Sychar there may have been a flowing spring, but Jesus had no equipment to reach that far down into the well. The woman thought Jesus was offering her a source of water that would not require the long trek to the well each day.

Question 5. Jesus certainly is not trying to embarrass the woman. He reveals her situation to do two things: to demonstrate his knowledge as the Messiah and to bring her to a fresh realization of her spiritual need.

Question 6. When the woman senses Jesus' intimate knowledge of her life, she tries to move the discussion to a safer topic, but something controversial enough to prompt a response from Jesus. The Jews believed (correctly according to Jesus) that the proper place for the worship of God was the temple in Jerusalem. The original temple was built by King Solomon and rebuilt after the exile into Babylon. The temple of Jesus' day was called the Second Temple or Herod's Temple since Herod the Great financed its expansion and beautification. The Samaritans continued to worship at the ruins of a rival temple they had built on Mount Gerizim (a hill visible from Sychar). The controversy over the proper place of worship was certain to stir comment from any Jew or any Samaritan.

Jesus answered her question honestly but then brought the flow of the conversation back to her own spiritual condition.

Question 7. Jesus was preparing the woman (and ultimately his own followers) to break away from the idea that God is locked within a church or temple. God seeks those who will worship him continually in their spirit and who will not be shackled with rules and empty tradition.

Question 8. The woman recognized that Jesus was a prophet because of his divine insight into the details of her life (v. 19). Jesus then took her further and revealed himself as God's promised Redeemer. All through the Old Testament God had promised to send a deliverer who would restore the fellowship with God that human sin had destroyed. The coming of the Messiah was a universal hope among the Jews and Samaritans. The woman responded to Jesus' revelation of himself with belief. The evidence that she believed is that she went into Sychar to announce her discovery to the people there (vv. 39-42).

Study 2. I Am the Bread of Life: Survival. John 6:25-51.

Purpose: To discover Jesus as the source of spiritual satisfaction.

Question 1. You may want to review the first part of John 6 to give your group the context for the claims Jesus made. This seems to be the same crowd that Jesus had fed the day before. Now they asked for another miracle and were divided in their opinion of who Jesus was and what they thought he should do for them. Also notice verse 52: "the Jews began to argue sharply among themselves."

Question 2. Physical nourishment is satisfied only temporarily, and we have to go through the process of seeking an adequate supply. The desire for spiritual satisfaction is a driving force of equal power. The only adequate source to meet that need is Jesus. We need to regularly draw from Jesus the life that sustains our spirits. The search for an adequate supply is no longer a difficulty either. The "bread" that our spirits long for is always available in abundance as we come to Jesus for his provision.

Question 3. The crowds in Jesus' day (just like many people today) wanted Jesus to perform some miracle and then they would believe. They forgot the miracle that they had witnessed just the day before! Jesus calls for faith before proof; human culture wants proof before they will even consider faith.

Question 4. Jesus, as the bread of life, provides the nourishment for our spirits that physical food provides for our bodies. Without food we weaken and die; without Jesus' life we weaken in our spiritual life and ultimately collapse. Just as physical food has to be eaten and absorbed, we have to draw on the word and power of Jesus as the source of our spiritual life. Other sources that promise spiritual life will prove to be empty or meager or fatal. Only Jesus can fully satisfy the longing of the human heart for a connection with God and his love.

Question 6. Jesus promises that he will never push away or ignore a person who comes to him in genuine faith. He has already promised to receive us before we come. He also offers assurance to the believer that he or she will be kept in God's love by Jesus' power and by the determination of the Father to save those who believe in his Son.

Question 7. The crowd could only comprehend what was natural and obvious. They knew Jesus as Joseph's son. They couldn't imagine that he was anything more than a human being like they were.

Question 9. If you have the time, divide the group into teams of two or three and give them poster board and markers. Ask each team (or each person) to choose the one claim made by Jesus in this passage that means the most to them. Print the claim on the poster board and decorate it with appropriate artwork. Have each smaller group share their choice with the entire group.

Study 3. I Am the Light: Direction. John 8:12-30.

Purpose: To comprehend Jesus' willingness to be the directing, purifying light in our lives.

Question 1. Jesus distinguishes between two realms, darkness and light. Each realm is inhabited by human beings—children of the darkness and children of the light. The dividing factor between these two realms is Jesus, the true light of the world. Children of the light will come to the light and will follow the light; children of the darkness will avoid the light and reject his grace. The world we live in belongs to the realm of darkness, and we are called to walk in Jesus' light and be light-bearers ourselves. Obviously, Jesus was using a metaphor to talk about spiritual realities. We are either followers of Jesus or lovers of spiritual darkness.

Question 2. Testimony given in court always had to be verified by the testimony of another. The Pharisees (members of a strict religious sect of Judaism) were saying that Jesus' claim alone was not enough to make it true. Jesus' response was that he always spoke with the Father's authority and approval. Therefore, whenever Jesus spoke, his testimony had to be accepted because the Father was his verifying witness.

Question 3. What we believe about Jesus is supported by several witnesses. The New Testament writers recorded accurately what Jesus said and did. The Holy Spirit within us affirms the truth of what we believe. Jesus' testimony is proven true not only by the Father's supporting witness but by the fact of Jesus' resurrection from the dead. The resurrection verifies that all of Jesus' claims about himself were true. If you have seekers or those who are seriously questioning the validity of Jesus in your group, you may want to do some reading in a good apologetic resource that will help you defend the authority of Jesus and the Bible.

Question 4. The Pharisees could only think of Jesus on a purely natural, earthly level (as in Jn 7:27). They were incapable and unwilling to consider that he might have had an eternal aspect. If they had been willing to believe that Jesus was God the Son, they would have known God the Father as well.

Question 5. Our pluralistic culture regards such a claim as narrow and dogmatic. Many people today want to believe that all religions lead ultimately to God—a position Jesus clearly rejects. He was speaking to a group of very religious, deeply sincere men but told them clearly that, without faith in him, they were lost.

Question 6. Not even Jesus' closest followers fully grasped who Jesus was until after his death on the cross and his resurrection from the dead. The cross is the fullest display of the glory of God and the love of God for lost humanity. The cross was also the first step for Jesus on the path back to the Father, completed in Jesus' resurrection and exaltation. Jesus came into the world to reveal the Father, and he revealed the Father's heart most clearly through his sacrificial death on the cross.

Question 7. The testimony of our lips is validated by the obedience of our lives. That doesn't mean we never fail but we handle sin and failure correctly. It is as people see Christ's love and holy character fleshed out in our lives that the testimony of our words begins to have an impact. Both parts are essential. Words without a life result in hypocrisy; a life without words is not enough to bring another person to faith.

Question 9. Jesus as the light provides direction and guidance. Light also exposes what needs to change. Children of the light also need to realize that light is not welcomed by those who are content to live in the realm of darkness.

Now or Later. If your situation permits, you could do the flashlight demonstration in the room or home where you have your study. Turn off the lights and demonstrate how light operates in the realm of darkness. When you lay the light down, it gives you light for a while (if you walk in its path) but you are soon walking again in darkness. Let the group voice the spiritual principles they learn from your demonstration.

Study 4. I Am the Good Shepherd: Security. John 10:1-21.

Purpose: To instill a sense of Christ's protection and provision for his followers.

Question 1. Jesus used an extended allegory in this passage to convey spiritual truth. Jesus acts toward us in the same way that a faithful shepherd acts toward his flock of sheep. The use of this familiar image (in Jesus' culture) helped his listeners connect more closely with Jesus and understand his teaching more clearly.

It might be helpful as the group answers this question to list the actions of the shepherd toward his sheep on a poster board or white board. You can underline or highlight the qualities the group thinks are most important in the person who "shepherds" their lives. Some group members may not want to have someone else shepherd them.

Be prepared to talk about why we may be like sheep at times and the advantages of trusting a caring shepherd.

Question 3. The thief or the wolf represents anyone who has a goal other than protecting and caring for the sheep. False teachers, greedy leaders, Satan—all fit the role of those who are more interested in themselves than in the sheep.

Question 4. Jesus was talking about his life of sacrifice and the ultimate gift of love on the cross. The good shepherd does whatever is necessary to provide for the sheep. Jesus' love is measured not simply by his provision of food and shelter but by his willingness to give his life for the sheep.

Question 5. The depth of Jesus' love for us is revealed by his spirit of voluntary sacrifice. Laying down his life is not something required of him or forced on him. He made a choice to become the ultimate sacrifice simply out of love for the sheep.

Question 6. Jesus' words created division in the crowd. Some were attracted and believed; some drew the conclusion that he was insane. His teaching requires a spiritual response. Some in the crowd were willing to receive his truth and some refused. Depending on the makeup of your group, you may see the same division of response to what Jesus said.

Question 8. Some group members may not feel comfortable sharing this answer with the whole group. You, as the group leader, can set a confessional tone by sharing your answer first.

Question 9. Jesus makes his love and acceptance clear before we ever become part of his flock. He promises his care and protection before we trust him to demonstrate his willingness to receive us. We are not asked to measure up to some impossible standard or to earn the shepherd's approval. Jesus simply asks us to hear his voice and follow him.

Study 5. I Am the Resurrection: Eternity. John 11:1-27.

Purpose: To strengthen our confidence in Jesus' power to bring life out of death.

Group discussion. As group members share their responses, encourage honesty and transparency. Do not judge or try to "correct" how a person felt toward God at a particular time. Allow even the difficult responses to prompt some serious reflection and thought.

Question 1. Jesus regularly spent time with Lazarus and his two sisters, Mary and Martha. (See Mt 21:17; Lk 10:38-42; Jn 12:1-3.) They apparently were very dear and trusted friends and were able to express themselves candidly to each other. Later in the passage even Jesus' enemies remarked about how much Jesus loved Lazarus when they saw Jesus weeping at Lazarus's tomb (Jn 11:36).

Question 2. These events took place during the final year of Jesus' ministry, a year of increasing opposition from the religious leaders in Jerusalem. His enemies had already tried once to kill Jesus (see Jn 10:31), and they were simply looking for another opportunity to remove him from the scene.

Question 3. If time permits, you may want to explore with the group why Jesus delayed his coming to Lazarus and what we can learn from that situation about why God may delay meeting a need in our lives.

Question 4. Jesus had previously raised people from the dead (Lk 7:11-15; 8:41-42, 49-56), but it's hard to know if Martha thought Jesus would do that for her brother. Later in the passage, when Jesus told the people at the tomb to move the stone that blocked the door, Martha was the one who protested that her brother's body would smell from decay. That protest seems to indicate that she did *not* expect Jesus to raise Lazarus from the dead.

Question 5. You, as a leader, or some in the group may want to defend God as others share their disappointments with God, but the point of the question is to give group members the permission to be honest about their struggles. Answers to those disappointments come only as we grow in our confidence in Jesus—the whole purpose of this study!

Question 6. Even though a Christian dies physically, we will continue to live beyond the experience of death. The body dies, but the spirit or soul remains alive in conscious fellowship with Christ.

Question 7. The one who believes in Jesus will never die the final, eternal death of separation from God forever. Jesus' statement is not a denial of physical death but a word of deliverance from the second death.

Question 8. Eternal life is not something we get when we die; it's what we receive when we believe. The Christian is born in a new way and receives God's gift of eternal life, a whole new kind of life.

Question 10. Jesus' power to bring life is not confined to physical death. Jesus can bring his life to a dead friendship or marriage. He can bring new life to a person who is "dead" in sin and failure. Jesus can restore life to a person who is controlled by alcohol or addiction.

Study 6. I Am the Way: Peace. John 14:1-14.

Purpose: To receive the peace that comes from knowing God through faith in Jesus.

Question 2. Jesus looks beyond the cross to the time of his ascension into heaven. While he is away, he will be preparing the Father's house for his followers. He will also be preparing his followers to join him in heaven. Verse 3 is one of the clearest statements from Jesus about his second coming.

Question 4. Thomas was still struggling with the fact that Jesus was leaving them. He still had a troubled heart, and he was not putting his trust in what Jesus had told them. His question opened the door for Jesus' claim in verse 6. Jesus pointed Thomas back to confidence in him alone as the remedy for a troubled heart.

Question 5. Our contemporary, pluralistic culture sees this claim as narrow and unenlightened. The cry for tolerance has come to mean acceptance. Christians in a secular society may tolerate all religions and support religious freedom, but tolerance does not mean that we regard all religions as true or of equal authority. Jesus did *not* teach that all religions lead to God. He claimed to be the only way.

Question 6. As Christians we believe that Jesus is God and that he speaks what is true. Therefore, when we say that Jesus is the only way to God, we are not the ones making that judgment. We are simply accepting and agreeing with what Jesus said. Spiritual truth is absolute. It's not just "true for me" while something else may be "true for you." Jesus is not one version of the truth; he is the truth.

Question 7. Philip wanted Jesus to show God to them and then it would have been easier to trust what Jesus was saying. Jesus responded by telling Philip that, if he has seen Jesus, he has already seen all that God is. The fullness of God's character is revealed in Jesus.

Question 8. Some Christians believe this verse teaches that Jesus' followers should do more miracles of power and healing than Jesus did. But if you examine the New Testament carefully, none of the apostles performed great numbers of miracles. None of them came close to the quantity that Jesus performed. What Jesus was saying was that his followers would do works of greater significance than his miracles. Jesus fed great crowds, but the people got hungry again. He stilled storms, but more storms followed. The Christian who, through their testimony about Jesus, brings another person to faith, however, is the channel for a work of God that has eternal significance. Jesus' followers have also seen far greater scope to their work than Jesus did. He spent his whole ministry in a tiny strip of land in the Middle East; Christians since then have taken his message to the world.

Question 9. Jesus promises to do whatever we ask in his name. That does not mean tacking a phrase on the end of a prayer. It means to ask in Jesus' place, to ask for what he would ask for in the same situation. If we are so in tune with God's character and will that we can pray as Jesus would pray, Jesus will do it. Jesus is also pointing to himself as the focus of prayer and the one with sufficient power to answer prayer. We can pray to Jesus in the same way we pray to the Father.

Question 10. This question gives you an opportunity to focus again on who Jesus claims to be in this passage and what he promises to do. The cure for a troubled heart is not just to pretend things are okay. The cure for a troubled heart is to exercise confident trust in who Jesus is and to believe that he will do what he has promised to do.

Study 7. I Am the True Vine: Purpose. John 15:1-8.

Purpose: To discover our purpose in the plan of God and to pursue that purpose with joy.

Question 1. The main vine provides nourishment and support to the branches. Without the vine, the branches quickly die. The branches provide the vine with fruit and leaves. Without the branches, the vine is unproductive.

Question 2. A biblical allegory (which is what Jesus is using in this passage) is designed to convey spiritual truth through common imagery. Allegories are similar in this respect to parables. Interpreters sometimes press too hard to find spiritual meaning in every small detail of the allegory, when the primary meaning is in the main elements of the allegory. As group members answer this question, try to keep the focus on the main points: the vine and the branches. It's possible to push the interpretation of the imagery too far.

Question 3. The Father takes action toward both kinds of branches. The branches that produce no fruit are removed. The discussion on this point can easily move to the issue of the security of the believer and whether genuine believers can ever lose their salvation. You will probably want to steer away from extensive debate on that issue and focus more directly on the content of John 15.

The Father doesn't ignore the branches that produce fruit. He actively works to prompt them to new levels of fruit-bearing. A more in-depth discussion of pruning will come in question 6.

Question 4. The "fruit" is sometimes interpreted as new converts to Christ. The problem is that branches on a vine are not said to be fruitful if they produce more branches. Branches are designed to produce grapes. The fruit God desires in our lives is the outward evidence of our true inward nature. Followers of Christ are called to display the character of the vine: the "fruit" of the Spirit (Gal 5:22-23).

Question 5. The Christian is not commanded to produce fruit. The only command is to remain or abide in Christ. To remain in Christ has both active and passive elements in it. On one hand, we simply rest and receive the life that flows to us from Jesus. On the other hand, we actively obey the command to abide or to remain in Christ. We have a part to play in maintaining the relationship with Jesus through prayer, listening to his Word, worship, obedience and faith. If we refuse to abide in him, the Father removes us. Whatever position the group members may hold on the issue of the security of the believer in Christ, they have to come to grips with what Jesus says in this passage.

Question 6. The disciples were facing a time of pruning or cleansing even as Jesus spoke these words. In a few hours, Jesus would be arrested, and the disciples would run. One would openly deny knowing the Lord. The Father may use a wide variety of ways to remove the things that hinder our spiritual growth. Some may hurt—loss, injury, failure; others may require patience and perseverance—loneliness, solitude, recovery from illness, separation. God's goal in these experiences is not to harm us but to stimulate a greater and deeper desire to remain close to Christ.

Question 8. The Christian's purpose in life is to bring glory to God by producing the fruit of Christlikeness in our lives. That purpose applies to every follower of Jesus no matter what our age, profession, social position, education, physical ability or level of spiritual maturity. It's a goal that constantly expands as we grow and mature in the Lord.

Question 9. Try to shape these answers to be as specific and practical as possible. To simply "remember my purpose each day" is too general. A better response is: "I will write out a statement of my purpose and put it on the bathroom mirror or on my cell phone where I will see it each day and be reminded of God's calling in my life." Sharing your purpose with another person is another way to cement its truth into your life. We can also incorporate a statement of purpose into our prayer life as we ask for Jesus' power to enable us to be productive branches.

Study 8. I Am the Alpha and Omega: Confidence. Revelation 1:8; 22:12-16.

Purpose: To examine Jesus' claim to be the sovereign Lord over human history and over our lives.

Introduction. The alpha and the omega are the first and last letters of the Greek alphabet. The idea behind Jesus' words is that he was present at the beginning of human history, and he will be the one who brings human history to a close—and he is actively involved at every point in between!

Question 1. In Revelation 1:8 the speaker is the Lord God, the Almighty; in Revelation 22:16 the speaker is Jesus. Equal claims are made by Jesus and the Lord God. This can mean that Jesus is the speaker in both verses and is, therefore, calling himself God, or it can mean that Jesus and the Lord God (the Father) are equal and can both make the same claim.

Question 2. Most people (including a lot of Christians) go through each day without one thought that Jesus might return and set in motion the final wrap-up of human history. The New Testament writers, however, consistently point to Jesus' soon return as a powerful motivation for holy living (1 Thess 5:4-8; 1 Jn 3:3). We also don't give much thought to our accountability to the Lord for what we do day after day. Christians are not saved by their good works, but we will receive rewards from Christ based on the faithfulness of our lives to him (1 Cor 3:10-15; 2 Cor 5:10).

Question 3. The Bible repeatedly claims that God is actively involved in overseeing events on earth. The entire human story is moving toward the conclusion that God has planned. God's sovereignty (his active control over human events) does not rule out or negate human responsibility or choice. God's sovereign plan includes human freedom and possible alternatives, but it still moves in the direction and toward the end that God desires.

Question 4. You will probably get widely differing viewpoints on this issue, and the purpose is not to respond at length to each one but to think about the possibilities that have been expressed. You might want to list the various views, and then decide which end-times possibilities are initiated by humans and which are initiated by God or by forces outside human control.

Question 5. The image of "washing their robes" implies being washed in the blood of Christ through faith in him (see Rev 7:14, for example). Those who by faith have trusted in Christ will have access to the tree of life (an image of eternal, joy-filled life in heaven) and to the heavenly city (a picture of our eternal dwelling with God).

Question 6. Jesus' description of those outside or excluded from the city implies that they are people who have not believed in Jesus and whose lives have not been changed by his grace. A genuine Christian may fail or sin at times, but their lives are not marked by habitual sin and disobedience to God (1 Jn 3:6). Those who continue to practice sin demonstrate that they do not know God.

Question 7. The successes and failures of daily life come to us as part of God's sovereign plan. His reign as King does not rule out our choices or decisions or the consequences of those decisions, but he is able to use every circumstance of life to build godly character in our lives. We can also be assured that God will ultimately accomplish all that he desires in us. He will not fail to bring us to spiritual maturity and Christlikeness.

Question 8. This is a good question for everyone's participation. Hopefully each group member's response will help you identify an area where they have grown in their understanding of who Jesus is.

Douglas Connelly is the senior pastor at Parkside Community Church in Sterling Heights, Michigan. He is also the author of Angels Around Us *(InterVarsity Press) and* The Bible for Blockheads *(Zondervan) as well as twelve LifeGuide® Bible Studies.*

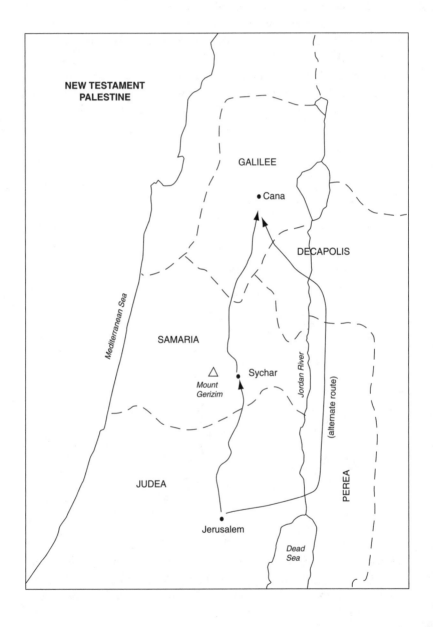

NEW TESTAMENT
PALESTINE

GALILEE

• Cana

DECAPOLIS

Mediterranean Sea

SAMARIA

△
Mount
Gerizim

• Sychar

Jordan River

(alternate route)

JUDEA

PEREA

• Jerusalem

Dead
Sea

OTHER LIFEGUIDE® BIBLE STUDIES BY
DOUGLAS CONNELLY

Angels
Daniel
Elijah
Encountering Jesus
Forgiveness
Heaven
John
The Lord's Prayer
Meeting the Spirit
Miracles

What Should We Study Next?

A good place to continue your study of Scripture would be with a book study. Many groups begin with a Gospel such as *Mark* (20 studies by Jim Hoover) or *John* (26 studies by Douglas Connelly). These guides are divided into two parts so that if twenty or twenty-six weeks seems like too much to do at once, the group can feel free to do half and take a break with another topic. Later you might want to come back to it. You might prefer to try a shorter letter. *Philippians* (9 studies by Donald Baker), *Ephesians* (11 studies by Andrew T. and Phyllis J. Le Peau) and *1 & 2 Timothy and Titus* (11 studies by Pete Sommer) are good options. If you want to vary your reading with an Old Testament book, consider *Ecclesiastes* (12 studies by Bill and Teresa Syrios) for a challenging and exciting study.

There are a number of interesting topical LifeGuide studies as well. Here are some options for filling three or four quarters of a year:

Basic Discipleship
Christian Beliefs, 12 studies by Stephen D. Eyre
Christian Character, 12 studies by Andrea Sterk & Peter Scazzero
Christian Disciplines, 12 studies by Andrea Sterk & Peter Scazzero
Evangelism, 12 studies by Rebecca Pippert & Ruth Siemens

Building Community
Fruit of the Spirit, 9 studies by Hazel Offner
Spiritual Gifts, 8 studies by R. Paul Stevens
Christian Community, 10 studies by Rob Suggs

Character Studies
David, 12 studies by Jack Kuhatschek
New Testament Characters, 10 studies by Carolyn Nystrom
Old Testament Characters, 12 studies by Peter Scazzero
Women of the Old Testament, 12 studies by Gladys Hunt

The Trinity
Meeting God, 12 studies by J. I. Packer
Meeting Jesus, 13 studies by Leighton Ford
Meeting the Spirit, 10 studies by Douglas Connelly